PIANO • VOCAL • GUITAR

THE TOBYMAC

2   Burn for You

9   Catchafire (Whoopsi-Daisy)

23   City on Our Knees

16   Get Back Up

32   Gone

38   Hold On

48   I'm for You

58   Lose My Soul

68   Made to Love

75   Me Without You

82   New World

90   Slam

104   Somebody's Watching

98   Steal My Show

ISBN 978-1-4803-0231-0

Hal•Leonard® CORPORATION
7777 W. BLUEMOUND RD. P.O. BOX 13819 MILWAUKEE, WI 53213

Visit Hal Leonard Online at
www.halleonard.com

BURN FOR YOU

Words and Music by TOBY McKEEHAN,
ROBERT MARVIN and JOSIAH BELL

Moderately fast

I'm a brand-new man, I'm a con-scious man, I'm a
up in a sweat; those ghosts in my head had a

man who's burn-in' for You. The mis-takes I've made have been chased a - way to the
grip, but I slipped on by. It's a whole new day as the dark-ness fades and the

bot-tom of the o-cean blue. I'm a brand-new man in a for-eign land, I'm a
sun's climb-in' in the sky. I con-cede, my Love, that I need Your love. I'm be-

Additional Lyrics

Rap: I'm a whole new guy with a whole new vibe,
Changed inside, more flame in the fire.
Can't stop, won't stop prayin' for desire.
Like the bunny on the screen, feel so energized.

Old shell gone without a trace, new face,
No more shortness of breath, new pace.
Live life now without a taste of the fear,
TobyMac, Double Dutch, now let the smoke clear.

CATCHAFIRE
(Whoopsi-Daisy)

Words and Music by TOBY McKEEHAN,
JOE BALDRIDGE and SOLOMON OLDS

Moderately fast

Ooh wah ooh, dum dum dit - ty. Here come the boy from the cap - i - tal cit - y.

Ooh wah ooh, dum dum dit - ty. Here come the boy.

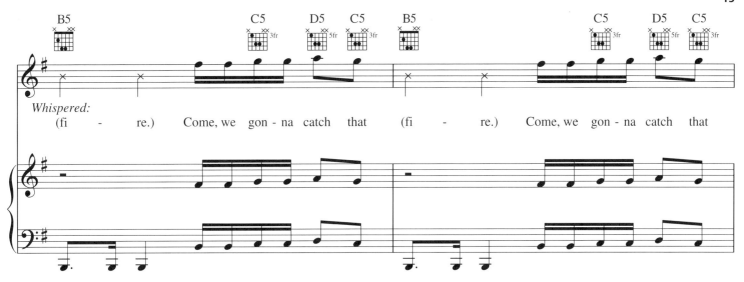

Additional Lyrics

Rap I:

Slackin' off like a bum, I'm feelin' ho hum.
I'm feelin' lukewarm like the water in my tub.
Started out and we was hot, looked up and now we're not.
We had that fire like we was boilin' in a pot.

Rap III:

Spark to a flame, I'm flippin' up my game.
I caught the fire and I'll never be the same.
So unexplainable I can't contain it, son,
And my retainin' it would only be a shame,
So let me hear you say . . .

Rap II:

. . . fire, I'm feenin' for a flicker,
Then we'll fan the flame up into something bigger.
Started out and we was hot, looked up and now we're not.
We gonna catch a fire, catch a fire for God.

Rap IV:

. . . heat, like the Kingston concrete.
There ain't no stoppin' the fire.
We're straight breakin' ground.
There ain't no coolin' this thing down.
We burnin' up and keepin' it krunk as we know how.
Hear me now, people.

GET BACK UP

Words and Music by TOBY McKEEHAN,
JAMIE MOORE, AARON RICE
and CARY BARLOWE

You turned a-way when I looked you in the eye, and hes - i - tat - ed when I asked if you were al - right.
You rolled _ out at the dawn-ing of the day, heart _ rac-ing as you made your lit - tle get-a-way.

CITY ON OUR KNEES

Words and Music by TOBY McKEEHAN,
JAMES MOORE and CARY BARLOWE

GONE

Words and Music by TOBY McKEEHAN
and CHRIS STEVENS

I told the girl that you should treat her like a la-dy and she told me all the things you did and it was shad-y, man.

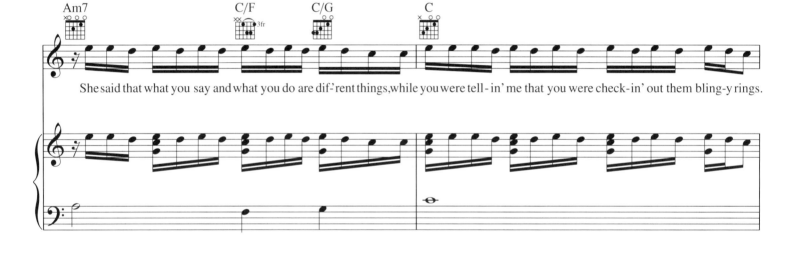

She said that what you say and what you do are dif-'rent things, while you were tell-in' me that you were check-in' out them bling-y rings.

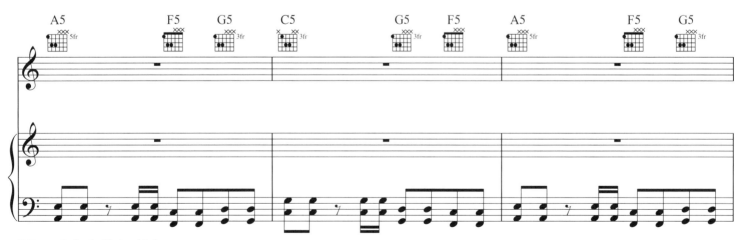

* Recorded a half step higher.

HOLD ON

Words and Music by TOBY McKEEHAN,
JESSE FRASURE and CARY BARLOWE

I'M FOR YOU

Words and Music by TOBY McKEEHAN,
AARON RICE and CARY BARLOWE

Heavily rhythmic, in 2

Tell me where it's hurt - ing. Are you burn - ing,

run - ning just to catch your breath, ___ and go - ing no - where?

LOSE MY SOUL

Words and Music by TOBY McKEEHAN,
MICHAEL RIPOLL and CHRIS STEVENS

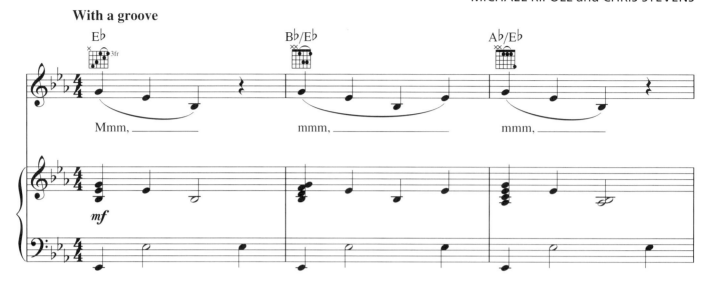

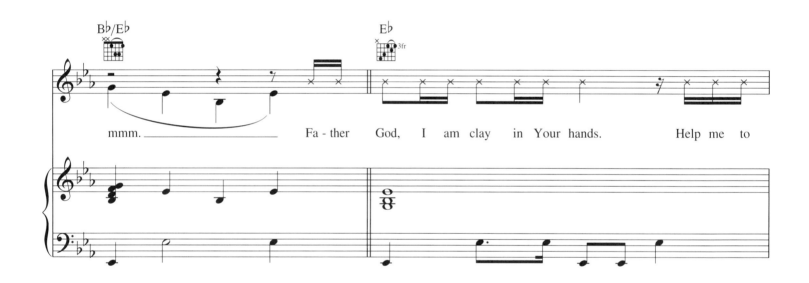

MADE TO LOVE

Words and Music by TOBY McKEEHAN,
CARY BARLOWE, JAMIE MOORE
and AARON RICE

ME WITHOUT YOU

Words and Music by TOBY McKEEHAN,
CHRIS STEVENS and DAVID GARCIA

NEW WORLD

Words and Music by TOBY McKEEHAN
and CHRIS STEVENS

The spell is weak-en-ing with ev-'ry breath He's breath-ing in, (and when He

and when He roars she can't ig-nore that He's our king a-gain.
roars,)

mp

(Spoken:) There!

Just beyond the lamppost!

I've seen, I've seen, I've seen a new _____ world. _____

into a new world, into Nar - ni - a.

In - to a new world, Nar - ni - a.

SLAM

Words and Music by TOBY McKEEHAN,
CHRIS STEVENS, JOE WEBER
and T-BONE

Hard Rock

Rap I *(See additional lyrics)*

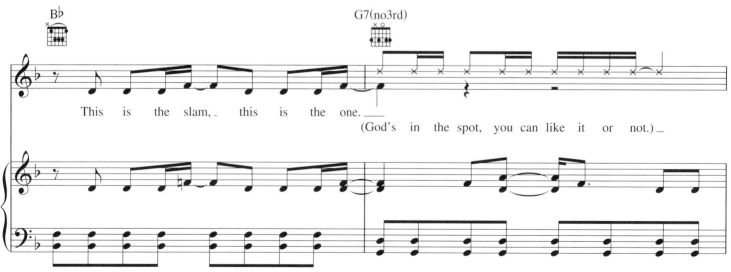

This is the slam,_ this is the one._
(God's in the spot, you can like it or not.)_

* Recorded a half step higher.

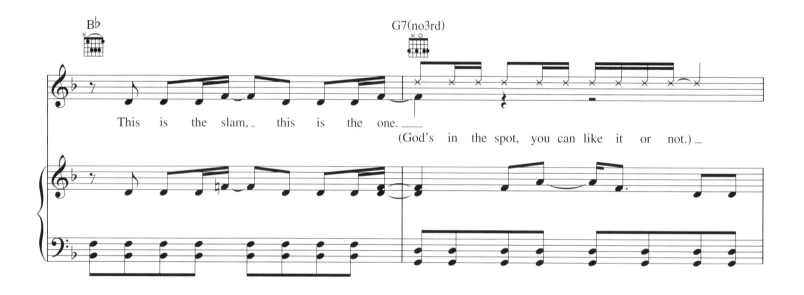

This is the slam,_ this is the one.___

(God's in the spot, you can like it or not.)_

This is the slam,_ this is the one.___

(We gon - na bring it like it ain't been brung.)

(Rap III ends)

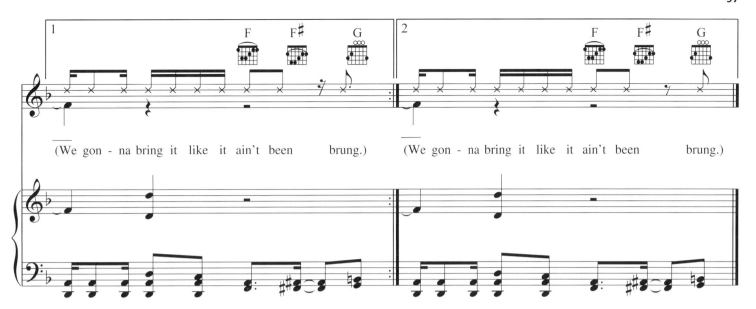

(We gon - na bring it like it ain't been brung.) (We gon - na bring it like it ain't been brung.)

Additional Lyrics

Rap I:

God's in the spot, you can like it or not.
So rip the knob off the volume when you give it a shot
And raise your hands as the slam starts to thicken the plot,
Openin' eyes to the lies of the enemies' lot.

So run like the wind from the sin of your past.
Keep your eyes on the prize when they put you on blast.
It's the Christ on the cross, it's humanity's shot.
It's a worldwide call to everything that we're not.

Rap II:

They came from the cities and towns all around
To see the long-haired preacher from the desert get down.
Waist high in water, never short on words, he said,
"Repent. The kingdom of Heaven can be yours."

But he stopped in the middle of his words and dropped
Down to his knees and said, "Behold, the Lamb of God.
He's the one, the slam, don't you people understand?
You're starin' at the Son, God's reachin' out His hand."

Rap III:

The Father slammed it like Shaq
For Latinos and Blacks
Packin' them straps,
And Caucasians hooked on Ecstasy and the crack,
Stacked the sins of this world to His body
And conquered evil and hell,
Then snatched the keys of death in one breath and unlocked the cell.
He rose on the third.
I'm tellin' you, partner, it's actual fact,
Just like TOBYMAC and Boney Soprano up on this track.
We slam dunkin' and keep it jumpin' like jumper cables
And keep the crowd rowdy like Jesus tossin' them temple tables.

STEAL MY SHOW

Words and Music by TOBY McKEEHAN,
CHRIS STEVENS and BRANDON HEATH

Moderately

An-oth-er cold __ night, an-oth-er late __ flight. It's al-most show - time and Di-verse Cit - y's wait-ing on me. We got a packed __ house; the crowd is call-ing out. They want the beat to drop, but what we real - ly need is You.

SOMEBODY'S WATCHING

Words and Music by ROCKWELL, TOBY McKEEHAN
and MICHAEL ANTHONY TAYLOR

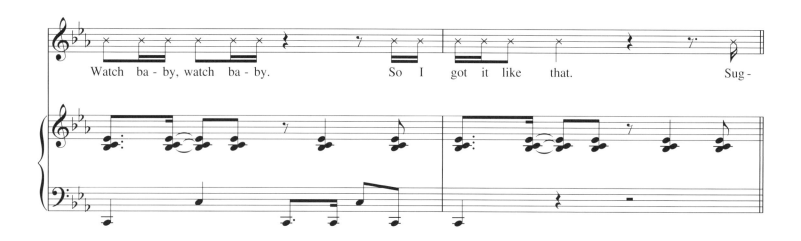

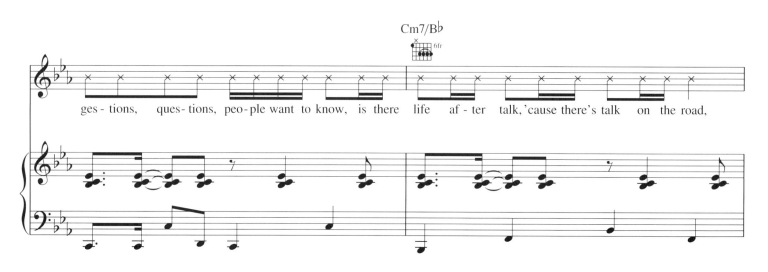